Mini Quilt Basics

1 Transfer the embroidery designs to the fabric blocks according to the Basic How-Tos on page 2. Stitch the designs. Press.

2 Follow the manufacturer's instructions to iron fusible webbing onto the backs of fabric scraps. Transfer the applique designs to the fabric pieces according to the Basic How-Tos on page 2. Cut out shapes and fuse them into place on project.

3 Use $1/4$" seam allowance throughout. To assemble the front of the mini quilt, sew sashing strips between the embroidered blocks, press seams open. Add the side strips, press the seams open. Add the top and bottom border strips. Press the seams open.

4 Lay the stitched front onto the backing fabric, right sides facing, and place the batting (if used) on the bottom. Sew the layers together around the outer edges, leaving a 4" opening along one side for turning. Turn the piece to the right side. Slip stitch the opening closed. Press.

5 Make a hanger with craft wire according to Wire Hanger Basics on page 23, or sew a 1" bone ring in place on the back at each of the top corners.

Rag Doll Book Cover on page 21, Pillowcase on page 22, Rag Doll Napkin on page 23, Rag Doll Frame on page 4.

Rag Doll Mini Quilt

You will need:
◊ Tea-dyed muslin blocks-
5" x $8^{1}/2$" for the doll
9" x 3" for the words
9" x $4^{1}/2$" for the wagon
◊ Red fabric -
Three 2" x $8^{1}/2$" strips for the sashing and side borders, one 2" x 9" strip for sashing, two 2" x $18^{1}/2$" strips for the top and bottom borders, one 12" x 19" piece for the backing
◊ Red embroidery floss   ◊ Red sewing thread
◊ 45" of Black craft wire for hanger   ◊ Scrap of Blue fabric
Follow the Mini Quilt Basics, above, to stitch and assemble the piece. Place running stitches around the outer edges of the blocks.

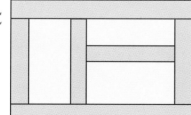

Pillowcases are great gifts!

How To Tea Dye

1 Dissolve 1 heaping Tablespoon of unsweetened instant tea in 1 cup of hot water.

2 Place the fabric blocks to be dyed in a heat-proof bowl and pour the hot tea mixture over them. Allow the fabric to steep in the tea until it is the desired shade of tan.

3 Remove the fabric from the tea and rinse the blocks with clear water. Roll the pieces in an old towel to remove excess moisture. Line or machine dry the blocks.

OPTION:
If you want to dye a lot of fabric, bring 4 cups of water and 4 one-quart tea bags to a boil. When the tea is cool enough to put your hands in it, submerge the fabric in the tea. Finish as above.

Frame Basics

1 Transfer the embroidery design to the fabric according to the Basic How-Tos on page 2. Stitch the design. Press.

2 Iron fusible webbing onto the backs of fabric scraps according to the manufacturer's instructions then transfer the applique designs to the fabric pieces according to the Basic How-Tos on page 2. Cut out the shapes and fuse them into position on the designs. Backstitch around the edges of each of the appliqued fabrics. Add additional embroidery to the appliques as desired.

3 Center the design over a piece of cardboard the same size as the frame opening. Fold the fabric edges to the back and glue or tape them in place to secure.

4 Add mat board edges cut to fit your frame opening with a window cut out for the design, or you may want to glue 1" strips of a complementary fabric around the edges of the mounted design before framing it.

Star Hanger on page 23, Star Book Cover on page 21, Santa Book Cover on page 21.

Flag Wall Hanging

You will need:
◊ 6" x 8" piece of muslin   ◊ Red embroidery floss
◊ Two 2" x 6" strips of Dark Blue fabric for the sides
◊ Two 2" x 10¹/₂" strips of Dark Blue fabric for the top and bottom borders
◊ 8¹/₂" x 10¹/₂" piece of Dark Blue fabric for backing
◊ Scrap of Dark Blue fabric for the star
◊ 40" of Black craft wire for the star hanger
Follow the instructions for Mini Quilt Basics on page 3 to finish.

Uncle Sam Frame

You will need:
◊ 5" x 7" Navy frame   ◊ 7" x 9" piece of muslin
◊ 5" x 7" piece of cardboard   ◊ Scrap of Blue fabric
◊ Red embroidery floss   ◊ Hot glue or tape

Snowman Frame

You will need:
◊ 8" x 10" Green frame   ◊ 10" x 12" piece of muslin
◊ 8" x 10" piece of cardboard   ◊ Red embroidery floss
◊ Red and Green fabrics   ◊ Hot glue or tape

Rag Doll Frame

Photo on page 4
You will need:
◊ 8" x 10" Red frame   ◊ 10" x 12" piece of muslin
◊ 8" x 10" piece of cardboard   ◊ Red embroidery floss
◊ Tan, White and Blue fabrics   ◊ Hot glue or tape

Rooster Frame

Photo on page 22
You will need:
◊ 5" x 7" Red frame   ◊ 7" x 9" piece of muslin
◊ 5" x 7" piece of cardboard   ◊ Red embroidery floss
◊ Hot glue or tape

Cheryl Haynes
Cheryl designs in many craft areas. For a brochure of her patterns, send $2.00 to: The Prairie Grove Peddler, 4705 Glenn Wesley Court, Columbia, MO 65202.

Tami Rudd
Tami's felt designs are only one of her crafting talents. She has been crafting and designing for 10 years and loves to work with wood, ceramics, fabrics and felt.

Ruler of the Roost

... Red Revival - © 2000 Design Originals, USA - Iron-on Patterns Are Reversed - Ink Is Permanent - Cut Out Design Before Using

Life is better
down on the farm

Friends, like heirlooms, are special treasures

Best Friends

A good friend
is one who comes in
when the whole world
goes out

Blessed are the purrer in heart

May the
magic
of Christmas
light up
your life

Take thyme along to smell the flowers the flowers way life's

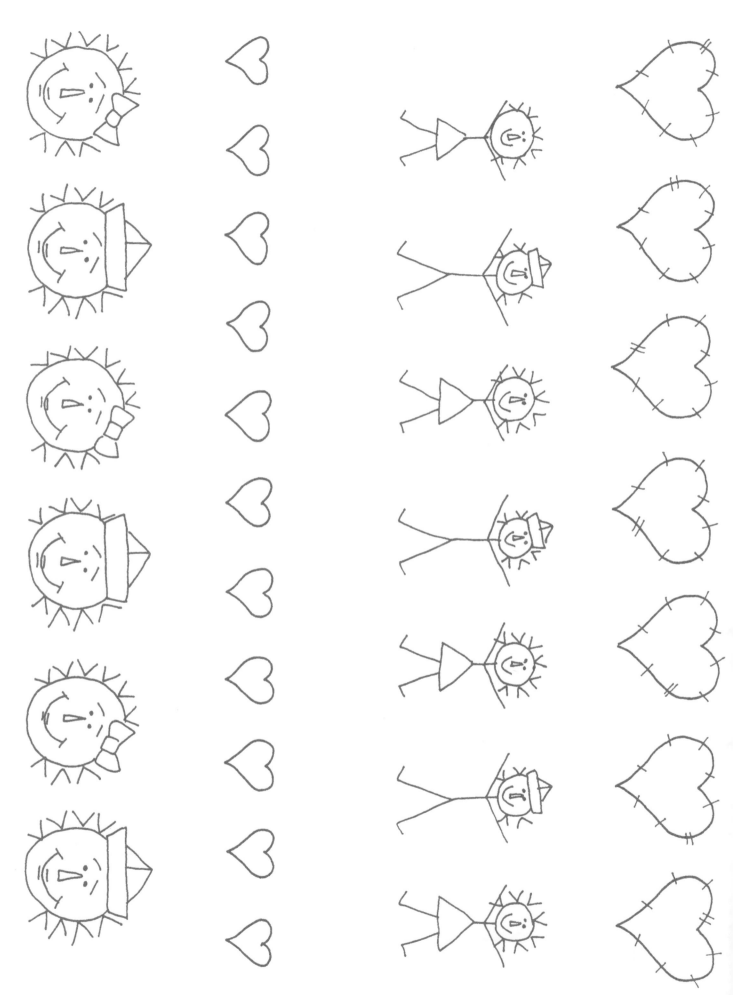

... Red Revival - © 2000 Design Originals, USA - Iron-on Patterns Are Reversed - Ink Is Permanent - Cut Out Design Before Using

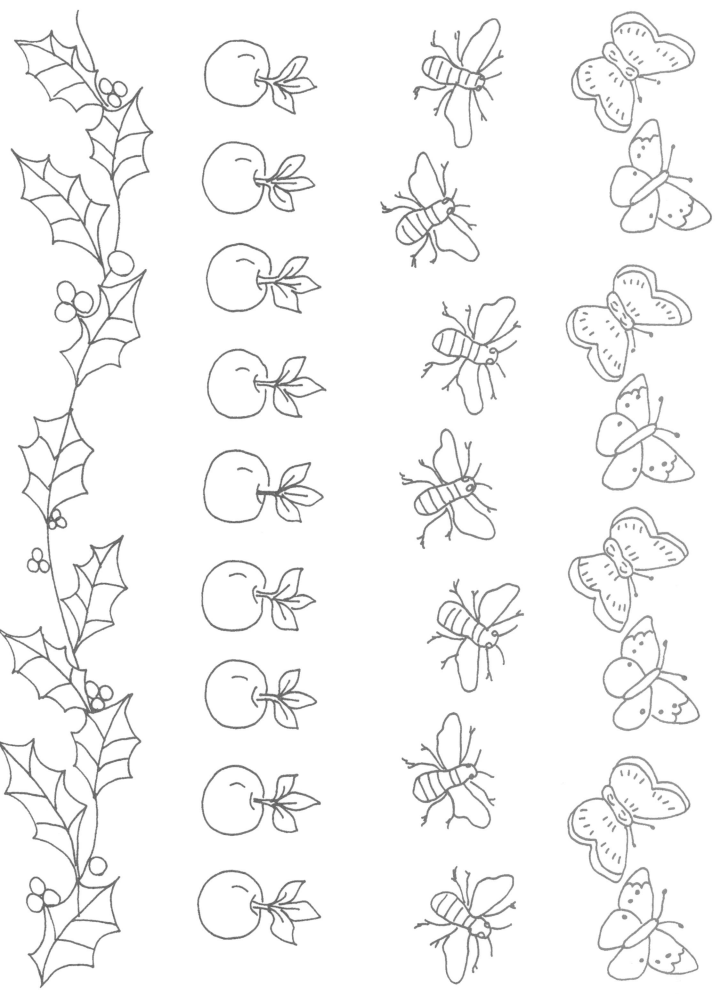

... Red Revival - © 2000 Design Originals, USA - Iron-on Patterns Are Reversed - Ink Is Permanent - Cut Out Design Before Using

Book Cover Basics

1 Close the book and use a tape to measure the book from the outer edge of the front cover around the spine to the outer edge of the back cover. Add 4" to this measurement for the end flaps that go over the edges of the covers.

2 Measure the height of the book. Add $1/2$" to $3/4$" to this measurement for the top and bottom margins.. Cut the felt according to your measurements.

3 Fold back 2" at the right end of the felt. Lay the closed book on the felt to align with the fold and centered from top to bottom. Mark the outer edges of the book with pins. Unfold the end flap.

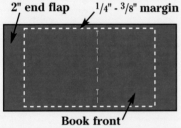

2" end flap **$1/4$" - $3/8$" margin**

Book front

4 Trace the patterns and transfer them to felt. Cut out the pieces and add buttons and stitching trim. Arrange the pieces on the book front area as shown in the photo. Glue or blanket stitch the pieces in place. Remove pins.

5 Fold back and pin the 2" flaps at each end of the felt. Blanket stitch across the top and the bottom edges of the book cover. Stitch through both layers of felt across the end flaps.

Star Book Cover

You will need:
◊ $4^{1}/2$" x $3^{1}/2$" composition or sketch book
◊ 9" x 12" sheet of Cranberry felt for the cover
◊ 2" x $2^{3}/4$" square of Ivory felt
◊ Scrap of Dark Blue felt for the star
◊ $3/4$" Cranberry button
◊ Black embroidery floss
Follow the instructions for Book Cover Basics to assemble the cover.

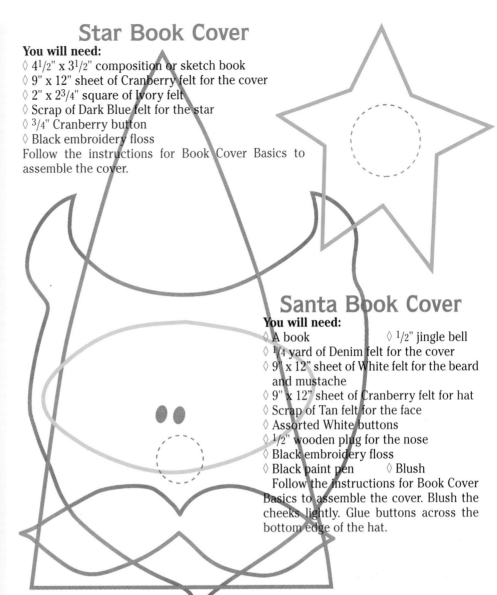

Santa Book Cover

You will need:
◊ A book   ◊ $1/2$" jingle bell
◊ $1/4$ yard of Denim felt for the cover
◊ 9" x 12" sheet of White felt for the beard and mustache
◊ 9" x 12" sheet of Cranberry felt for hat
◊ Scrap of Tan felt for the face
◊ Assorted White buttons
◊ $1/2$" wooden plug for the nose
◊ Black embroidery floss
◊ Black paint pen   ◊ Blush
   Follow the instructions for Book Cover Basics to assemble the cover. Blush the cheeks lightly. Glue buttons across the bottom edge of the hat.

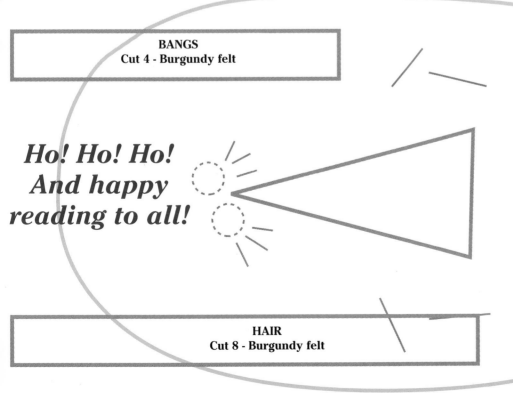

BANGS
Cut 4 - Burgundy felt

Ho! Ho! Ho! And happy reading to all!

HAIR
Cut 8 - Burgundy felt

Rag Doll Book Cover

You will need:
◊ Photo album
◊ $1/2$ yard of Navy felt
◊ 9" x 12" sheet of Tan felt for the face
◊ 9" x 12" sheet of Burgundy felt for the hair, bangs and nose
◊ Two 1" x 10" torn strips of Blue and White checked fabric for the hair bows
◊ Two 9mm round Black buttons for the eyes
◊ Navy, Tan, Burgundy and Black embroidery flosses
◊ Blush
   Follow the Book Cover Basics, above, to cut the Navy felt, *except*, allow 4" (instead of 2") at each end of the cover for the end flaps. Blush the cheeks. Glue the fabric bows in place.

Chicken Mini Quilt

You will need:

◊ Tea-dyed muslin blocks -
one 8$^{1}/_{2}$" square for block No. 1,
one 5$^{1}/_{2}$" x 8$^{1}/_{2}$" piece for block No. 3,
one 6$^{1}/_{2}$" x 7$^{1}/_{2}$" piece for block No. 5

◊ Plain muslin blocks -
one 5$^{1}/_{2}$" x 8$^{1}/_{2}$" piece for block No. 2,
two 6" x 6$^{1}/_{2}$" piece for blocks Nos. 4 and 6

◊ Assorted Green print fabrics -
two 2$^{1}/_{2}$" x 8$^{1}/_{2}$" sashing strips for the top row
two 2$^{1}/_{2}$" x 6$^{1}/_{2}$" sashing strips for the bottom row
three 2$^{1}/_{2}$" x 22$^{1}/_{2}$" strips for sashing between the rows and the top and bottom borders
two 2$^{1}/_{2}$" x 21" strips for the side borders, one 24" x 28" piece for the backing

◊ 24" x 28" piece of batting   ◊ Red embroidery floss

Follow the instructions for How to Tea Dye, on page 2, for the muslin blocks. Follow the instructions for Mini Quilt Basics, on page 3, to assemble the project.

Chicken Towel

You will need:

◊ Red checked dish towel   ◊ Red embroidery floss

1. Iron fusible webbing onto the back of the muslin then transfer the applique design to muslin according to the Basic How-Tos on page 2.

2. Cut out the shape and fuse it into position on the towel. Backstitch around the edges of the appliqued fabric. Add additional embroidery along the lines of the design. Press the finished piece.

Chicken Pillow

You will need:

◊ 12" square of muslin
◊ $^{1}/_{2}$" yard of wedding ring chenille
◊ Red embroidery floss
◊ Red fabric dye
◊ Polyester fiberfill
◊ Red sewing thread

1. Transfer the embroidery design to muslin according to the Basic How-Tos on page 2. Stitch the design. Press.

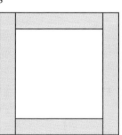

2. Follow the manufacturer's instructions to dye the chenille. When the chenille is dry, cut one 18" square for the backing. Cut two 4" x 12" pieces for the top and bottom borders. Cut two 4" x 20" pieces for the side borders.

3. Use $^{1}/_{2}$" seam allowance throughout. Sew the side borders in place, press the seams open. Add the top and bottom strips and press the seams open.

4. Sew the pillow front to the backing, right sides facing. Leave a 6" opening along one side for turning. Turn to the right side. Stuff pillow firmly with fiberfill. Sew opening closed.